Word in EdgeWise

Brad Rose

Červená Barva Press
Somerville, Massachusetts

Červená Barva Press
P.O. Box 440357
W. Somerville, MA 02144

http://www.cervenabarvapress.com

Visit the bookstore at:
http://www.thelostbookshelf.com

Production: Allison O'Keefe
Cover: Hannah Rose

ISBN: 978-1-950063-69-7

LCCN: 2024939161

"The ugly may be beautiful, the pretty, never." — Paul Gauguin

"Every view of things that is not strange is false." — Paul Valéry

CONTENTS

Word in EdgeWise

Custody

It's like that time I was taking the bus to Vegas with Misty so we could shoot craps. She looked like she was dressed by Satan. We were smoking. Don't recall if they were Camels or Kools. Misty said, *What do you think I should wear to court next week, Ray?* I said, *Depends on whether you want custody of your kids, or not.* Misty looked out the window like she was trying to conserve energy, burn fewer calories. She was wearing too much perfume, but I liked it. Without saying anything, she stared out the window for at least the next five miles. Then she said, *I hear you, Ray*, like she was closing the lid on a kid's coffin. I asked the bus driver how long until we reached Vegas, and he told me we had about an hour's ride ahead of us-- give or take an hour. He smiled a bus driver's smile into the rear-view mirror. The lady in the seat in front of us was wearing a flame-red wig. I think she was Chinese or Italian. Like I said, these days, who can you trust?

The Hurried Valley

Nearly died of too much weekend. Even if you think you've got only one symptom, you've probably got the whole disease. Like a bloodhound who's lost the scent, you have to learn to adjust your goals. I thought I saw a face in the trees, but it was just my pareidolia acting up. Bruegel or Bosch? It's bad, but it won't kill you. My half-sister arrived with a basket of rented food. Usually it doesn't agree with me, but here in Purgatory Park, I feel like a total bro, for sure. That's why I told her, *Appreciate each hand clapping in the applause. You never know when it's going to be too late to benefit from exercise.* But it's a balancing act. Your heart beats all the time. Six of one, a half-dozen of the other. Pretty soon you've grown eyes in the back of your head and the mountains crawl toward you, like a hunter on his knees, the dark of the approaching valleys, black and smooth as a panther's flank. You'd like to think they only toy with you, but you've never run as fast as you're running now, panicked prey fleeing the valley of the shadow of death. By the way, aren't those fantastic snakes? But don't take my word for it. Decide for yourself. No rush.

Dishonorable Discharge

While I was getting the poison out of my body, I accidentally started a fire in the bathroom sink. Maybe it was a just a coincidence? It's hard to know for sure, especially without witnesses. Chemicals burn a lot faster now, than they did when I was a kid. Last night, I slept like a wild animal, killed. Around three-thirty, woke up thinking out loud. Maybe it was too loud. Smoked a cigarette, counted my veins. The girl in the next apartment---I think she's a drummer in a band. She's got a military haircut, only bluer. Some people are what they aren't. They say shrapnel stays hidden in your body, like a secret. If you don't tell people about it, if you don't limp, how will they know? That girl's hair is bluer than a movie star's eyes. She's paler than a glass of milk. I try not to over-think it. Although we've never met, I've been in her apartment. More than once. Pretty sure she doesn't have boyfriend. At least, not yet.

Lightning

My words begin talking before I know what to say, but they're just words about talking. My teeth are asleep, time is rearranging my cells. Subconsciously, I'm quite tall. I hate to disagree with you, because I'm a 'yes' man, but I have no choice, it just turned out this way. Maybe it's because I was informed, not consulted? Of course, the angels are sad whenever the dead take risks, but there can be no light without darkness. Have you noticed how the countryside is green and slow, like it's taking sleeping lessons. I'd love to throw some money at it. Everything is absolutely relative around here, like an orphan's family tree. Since my sister's electrocution, I don't swim in lakes. I don't drink water. I prefer to sleep in my car. But enough about me; how are you doing?

Forgiveness

You and I have never met. It's probably just a coincidence. Yesterday, I looked through the blinds and I saw a stranger in the back yard. He wasn't doing much; just holding down the fort. Although he was quiet as a caterpillar, I could see his lips moving. I don't think it was the kind of song a bird sings. Sometimes I remember things that didn't happen. But not always. It's a miracle that guy in the newspaper last week survived his first lethal injection. The wife of the murder victim said she forgave the killer because she knew Jesus had, but he died later, anyway. An eye for an eye, and tooth for a tooth. It's so hard to make the world a better place. His lawyer was on TV last night. I never saw a lawyer cry, before. He said the state had sentenced the wrong man to death. The judge had ignored the DNA evidence. At least Jesus and the murdered man's wife were on the same page. It's always good when people see eye to eye.

Hidden Beauty

Every time I re-dream my arrest, I de-materialize. Like an anesthetized patient, I'm here and I'm not. I try to lock myself up, like a stray dog, but usually I lose my taste for poison before the cage door shuts. Jerome says I'm like a goldfish in a mall fountain, I'm caught in the indoor undertow. I wish I had a beach house. A river means nothing to me, at least not since I overheard those hidden conversations in the hospital waiting room. Now, I'm working from home, so I can spend more time having ideas. To the untrained eye, some wolves appear angrier than others. It's a long ride uptown, but it's worth it. It's never too late to start planning for your future. When I get off the bus, I'll be sure to thank the driver. That's the beauty of a sawed-off shotgun.

The Trouble in Retail

I need to spend more time in my basement, although even in the daylight, I can't see my own eyes. Lucinda says they're dark and distant, like someone driving through a tunnel toward a dead man's address. Yesterday, I told the boss I voted myself a raise. He thought that was funny. When I got home from work, I fell asleep on the couch. I couldn't tell whether the people in my dream were watching me, or if I was watching them, but I wasn't afraid because I counted my thoughts and they added up to an even number. Same as on weekends. Before he quit, my lifestyle coach said that he read about a man who discovered a two-headed butterfly. He wasn't sure how many antennae it had, but I'll bet it wasn't easy with all that incoming information. I'm not superstitious, but I know for sure most animals can't keep a beat. Let me tell you something. I don't like my job. The customer's always right, and there're just too many things you're not supposed to think about. Or scream.

Questions

Don't you hate questions? Me too. Dixie says questions are like sleepwalking, only more confusing--- like being stuck with only 99 cents in your pocket, between a convenience store and a pawnshop. Last week, I memorized the palm of my left hand. Not just the lifeline, but the whole palm. Lately, there've been a lot of rumors floating around. Of course, I don't pay any attention to them. If anything goes wrong, I know someone will notify my next of kin. On Tuesday, the radio said a judge complained that the police had given the coroner the wrong body. Imagine that. Must have been a real mix-up. Yesterday, Dixie and me were walking down by the 7-Eleven on Highway 6. As a cop car passed, Dixie asked, *When are you going to marry me, Roy?* I told her to finish her Dr. Pepper and stop giving me static. Dixie always says that after we get a little money together and stop living on the street, we should get married, have a real wedding. She's only half cute. Her eyes are different colors, but she's been faithful as a Collie. We've been together now, for almost two weeks, and she only tried to run away once. I wonder if she'd marry me if she knew I was the one who killed her first husband. I'd have told her all about it, but she never asked.

Like Snakes

I can't be sure who's telling you this, but the only part of a song worth listening to is the end, although I wouldn't be caught dead there if you paid me. It's the profit motive. In branding, they say it's all about the experience, but for better or for worse, it just boils down to the animals you eat. After a near death experience, it's vital to seem to be alive. You're known by the company you keep. Fast forward to the ugly pretty part. Under the sky's silent vowel, desire is the music that's always on. God is not dead. Unfortunately, there are no pistols allowed in church.

With her back to the confessional, mom said, *Your good luck tattoos won't keep you out of prison this time, son.*

I said, *Even if they aren't snakes, let them hiss.*

Nebraska

Early Sunday morning, just outside Hazard, the local farmers ganged together in their John Deeres to mow down the crop circles. The ones no one ever talked about. Then, they got good and drunk, before setting off for town in their Ford F-150s, to attend church.

Later that day, as you and I stood on your sagging front porch, skeletal lightning jittered in the distance—white blades stabbing at silver bones in a tense, gray sky. *It's just like the summer day my little sister disappeared*, you said, matter-of-factly. You looked so automatic and angular, like a splinter of God. *It's not that dangerous. Sure, there are spikes, but just little spikes. Anyway, they're still a long ways off.*

Then, in a voice hollow as a doll, you added, *We can't know why things happen. Not why they really happen. We just can't know.*

Love's Levitation

Although my body is an anchor, it's beginning to float. The darkness is a dim, fragile music. When I speak, things unhappen. If you listen, carefully, you may hear voices in my skin. There are different kinds of secrets. They conceal something no one knows, the way a dream conceals sleep from the sleeper. Like rain, it's nothing personal. It occurs to me there has been a change of address. I am closer now to a beginning, a storm without lightning or clouds. The air is loneliness. Birds fall from the flesh of the sky. I think only of you.

Bank Job

Yesterday, I got a call from Anonymous. Told me I should shave off my mustache so I wouldn't be recognized. It's too bad you can't eat every time you're curious. Last night, I dreamed of insomniac alligators. They were hung-over. One of them had chrome teeth. Another one said, *When you wake up, we'll be back.* If only my clothes would stop talking in my sleep. Sometimes their questions get stuck in my head. I keep meaning to do something about it. Luella is a lot prettier than my better half, but she's the evil kind of smart. She says things I don't understand, but it's not her fault, she didn't invent the words. We walked up to the first teller and Luella yelled, *Everybody get down on the floor.* You'd be surprised how beautiful a day it was. At first, it didn't sound anything like gunfire.

Demographic

The dead are busy dancing, although looks can be deceiving. To play it safe, I'm bankrolling the opposition. Thanks to my dialect coach, now even the plants understand me. Still, it never hurts to re-calibrate your survival instinct. I used to be a genius, but my chromosomes prematurely wore out in the lachrymose airwaves. Instead of repeating the mistakes of the past, I surrendered my hopes of playing first violin in the orchestra of the absurd. My parole officer assured me that it's easy to spot an unlucky skyscraper, although, like sad-eyed clown art, you never want too much of a good thing. Research shows that the people most affected by the death penalty are raised in similar zip codes. At first, this seemed funny, but they're not laughing anymore.

It's Hard to Get Ahead

Brainwashed the dishes. Now, I'm looking for money in large amounts and small denominations. Jesus says I'm a very legible person, but Raven says I don't have enough string to fly a kite. OK, so maybe I am still working out the kinks. This week they called off the weekend, so I'll just work right on through, at least until those Japanese Martians land. I'll wear water skis if I have to. I've heard hollow chocolate Easter bunnies really can work up an appetite. After all, you are what you eat. Of course, you can't trust everything they teach you in hairdressing school. To make up the deficit, I practiced my danceable moves in broad daylight. Before I knew what was happening, the cops asked me to leave. That nearly killed me. I love this country like the back of my hand. Can't count the number of times I've tried to set it on fire.

Free Parking

He rolled up all the windows and drove the car into the lake. Although it wasn't a very big car, it immediately began to sink to the mossy bottom.

With his lungs filled with what easily could have been his final breath, he pushed open the driver's-side door, and just as he always did, squeezed out into the vague, green water, propelling himself upward like a skittering bubble toward the lake's bright surface.

As he began to swim toward the deserted shore, he wondered if he would ever stop doing things just for the hell of it. He wondered if this might be the last car he'd steal and sink here, in the Maine woods?

Reaching shore, he climbed out of the chilly water, and surveyed the surrounding pines. The still trees, like unsuspecting gazelle, seemed to graze quietly at the water's edge. The vacant air, pure, buoyant, pointless.

It All Depends

Admiring the corporality of animals, we're parked in the ghost car. I have an indoor question. How many misspelled thoughts must I have, anyway? There's nothing more beautiful than wanting the impossible to be true, especially when it is. Time passes faster in the mountains, than by the sea. Like a drowned body, the sky's blue prairie floats overhead. Wind light as confetti. Maybe we should take a drive to the beach; go for a swim? I don't want to give away the ending, but I can tell you it's a beauty. No one attends their own funeral. Know what I'm saying? By the way, that outfit looks good on you. Although, it all depends on how you look at it.

On the Same Page

I eat the television steaks. When nobody's looking, I compliment my teeth. I've tried to discover which haircut is best for me, but I have a nervous tic. Whenever I have a question, I ask the internet. It's making the world a better place. Quiet as fingerprints, my blood has an invisible plan for me. Thank goodness for reincarnation. Yesterday, I started talking in an extinct language, but I didn't get any credit for it. The dead are so unfair. I'm tired of finishing my sentences, so as soon as I find my other hat, I'm going to give myself a new nickname. They tell me I don't remember the crash, but I can perform card tricks better than any of the nurses at the clinic. It just takes focus. Meanwhile, I'm going to stay here and hold down the fort. Those insects stay in your blood a lot longer than you think. Besides, I just wanted to make sure we're still on the same page.

Curious

Once I nearly fell off Riley's houseboat and drowned. Now, I'm going to get my pants altered. Took the muscle relaxant. It's nearly noon, but my hands are still near my fingertips. They say I'm adjusted, but not well-adjusted. Sometimes my skin melts off my face. Last night the sky gave me the silent treatment, but if you're like me, you always keep a bag packed, under the bed. You never know. Driving out on Tunnel Road, usually I don't miss myself until it's too late. Riley was like that, too. I loved him like a brother. It happened on Good Friday. I don't trust the county sheriff's office. That's why I asked the judge, *Was he found hanged or did he commit suicide?* What was Riley even doing in jail, anyway?

After Our Trip to Bank of America, Melinda and I Make Plans to Celebrate

Got to celebrate. Made an appointment for my next tattoo. Either blue barbed wire or red hatchet blades. Melinda offered to hypnotize me. I just love that girl.

Sure, I'd like to make a full recovery, but you can't back up that train. It's not how things are done around here.

Melinda told me she thinks Jesus is kind of cute. She asked, *"If there's a flood, should we swim toward or away from New Jersey?"*

I told her, *"Honey, it's really a good thing you didn't shoot both those guards."*

Same Old Story

Yesterday, in the backyard, I had to rip the encyclopedia out the monkey's hands. I don't know how many times I've told him he shouldn't read while cutting the lawn. Too dangerous. Then, Miguel came around the side of the house and said all the furniture was on fire. I yelled, *Not again*! American cheese, Canadian bacon, French toast; no wonder no one gets along these days. The junipers stood there, green and grinning like they always do, and I said to Miguel, *What are you looking at*? I don't know why I even try anymore. A heard of free-range clouds scuttered across the oblivious sky, heading toward somewhere important. The wind was light as day-old perfume, when Jasmine called me to ask about the happily ever after. Evidently, it hadn't arrived on time, so I reminded her that most of the cosmos is composed of invisible matter and said, *You're probably not looking for it in the right place.* Jasmine says I'm all trees, and no forest, that I have only temporary tattoos, but I've started thinking like a magician and making the best of my barbed wire face. Good looks aren't everything. Most people are below average. Of course, it's always summer on the sun and we all agree dollars are money. It's a no brainer. Miguel came back around to the front, where I was practicing my charisma, to say that the artificial intelligence had broken and we were going to have to make our own mistakes the old-fashioned way. I pointed out that the observables had disappeared and it was probably too late for the future to catch-up. Miguel said he'd had it up to here, didn't want to be famous anymore, got on his scooter, and left for parts unknown. I returned to my magical thinking and enjoying the anesthesia of my own company. I'm a humanitarian. I oppose human rights for monkeys, robots, and farm equipment. Like the Bible says, *Just as you sow, you shall reap.*

Ghost Instinct

I took the westerly pill and tried to get out of the wind. You said, *All we're doing is driving around the block, again and again*. One burning earthquake, and the trees, like trapped animals uncaged, head south for the winter. Am I the only one asking questions around here? As if it's accomplished with razor blades. Each obstacle creates a desire. Bone yearns for flesh, sea for sky. Yesterday, a body was found, no signs of struggle, limp limbs relaxing in the calm quantum. A ghost wind listened to its own swallowed scream. The tamed mouth seeks a feral kiss. You have a taste for carrion.

Ants

Tiny feet scurry toward the tunnels of home. Like motorists crying and driving. The sky is asleep, the day hourless. If they could speak, I'm sure they would ask, *Where are the bachelorettes*? but they're carrying little boulders in their jaws, the way a lion carries an impala by its broken neck. I wish they would relax. They have so much potential. Their hurried lives. As though they belong to someone else.

The Main Reason I Didn't Leave a Forwarding Address

Since I got an 'A' on my Turing test, it doesn't bother me that I can't hear my hair growing at night. Of course, I enjoyed the helicopter ride and the dog sledding, but the problem with my dead relatives is that they are still alive. There's something *je ne sais quoi* about their persistent yodeling, but, like a phantom limb, I can't quite put my finger on it. My physician say's as soon as I get better, it'll be OK to pawn my invisibility cloak. He says I shouldn't be bashful; everyone has a body beneath their clothes. I wanted to ask him, *What use is a fire escape without a fire*? but, I can tell you, naked or nude, he's not the kind of person who likes to take turns missing the boat. Of course, like Pa always said, it's not polite to scratch your itchy trigger finger in public. Don't bother coming back till you're dead.

That's Just the Kind of Guy I Am

I'm reading my mind. Hope nothing bad happens. Tammy says I'm clairvoyant, but I'm tired of talking about things before they happen. Yesterday, I spent the day sport-honking in traffic and avoiding the cops. I was surprised how easy it was. After I sell off my ammo collection, I'm going to retire early, so I can churn out a couple of country hits and never have to answer the phone again. Fortunately for my doctor, my blood is brightest in the dark. He said if I want to see blood, I don't need to cut myself. Last week, Tammy warned me about the 4th dimension. She said, even if I'm living in a parallel universe, it's hard to know what it's parallel to. That's probably why I can't remember things. At least I can walk on my hands. I make it look romantic. It's a gift. By the way, I'm pretty sure I was nowhere near that shooting at the mall. The newspaper said it all happened so fast.

Invitation to Sunrise

Tuesday, just before sunset, I drove past a guy holding a sign, *Will work for food*. Then I passed a billboard advertising Painless Surgery, and thought, *Can a person kill himself to get the insurance money?* The doctor's billboard picture wasn't too friendly. His head was larger than a car, and he smiled like a fish. I tried to keep in mind that the experimental results in mice don't always apply to humans.

A few streets later, I noticed a woman walking six dogs on single leash. The woman was short as a nail. The leash was a taut chain she held with both hands. Not one of the dogs was small. As the rain slowed, I could see she her jerky movements were making a busy tunnel in the wet air. I couldn't see her face. I wondered if she was pouting. The rain stopped, and everything smelled like wet cardboard.

Wednesday, my sister, JoJo, called to say that she's out of ammunition. Like the closest revolver grabbed, JoJo married a gun store owner, who was twice her age. The day before her wedding, I told her, one day, she would regret it, but she didn't believe me. Last June, they found her husband's dead body in a Best Western. He was naked. The police said the scene had been made to look like a suicide, but he didn't look unhappy. The room had two twin beds. None of the complementary bars of soap had been used.

After my call with JoJo, I decided now is as good a time as any to spend a few days with my cousin, Reuben, in Monroeville. He's got a house with a spare bedroom. Once, he was shot while he was transferring prisoners, but just that once. He always says that after that, he's not been afraid of anything. I don't think he likes me. I like his wife. Maybe a little too much. I told him every man is entitled to his opinion. Even a 2nd cousin.

Now, as I get in the pickup and turn onto the interstate, I notice the day is gray and low, like it's about to snow concrete. I drive with one hand and, with the other, I eat a left-over Egg McMuffin. I start thinking about my cousin's wife. She's got skinny knees, but she's pretty. She'd look better in glasses, but what can you do? Nobody's perfect.

Half-way there, a car passes me on the left. It's traveling about 120 mph. A few minutes later, I pass its wreck on the side of the road. I see the flames stretching up like desperate fingers toward an indifferent sky, the clouds of black smoke look like bags of steel wool on fire. The speed of everything is relative. I hear sirens on the highway behind me. It's hard to remember everybody's birthday.

When I get to Reuben's house it's almost sunset. The light is hushed like a secret. I recall that Reuben's not really a cop, he's a prison guard. His wife comes out of the house alone, and walks up the driveway to my tuck. I don't know why she married him. I don't think she knows either.

I roll down the window and say, *Hey*. She says *Hey* back. *Reuben's not here, he's at the bowling alley with his friends*. I notice her slippers are dying the wet snow, pink. She says, *Do you want to come inside*?

I remind myself, *Each second it's sunrise somewhere new in the world*.

No Immediate Report of Death or Injuries

I'm lying in the middle of the road. No, honestly. It's uncanny how much you can remember amid morning traffic. After all, are we friends, or just friends of friends? Like in the animal kingdom, it depends on who eats whom. Wednesday night, it got so dark. Did you see it? Me either. Felix called and apologized for dialing the wrong number. After he hung up, I tried to call him back, but it was anybody's guess, and nobody answered in a strange voice. That's the down side of nighttime lip-reading. For a long time, I was afraid that I was worrying about all the wrong things, but Mr. X says it's more important to deceive others than it is to deceive yourself. Can't tell you how many times I tried to hit that fly with a hammer. By the way, I've always wanted to tell you that you smell pretty as a bag of fresh groceries. No problem. As soon as my check clears, I'll call you.

Debt

I magnetized myself. Now, I'm afraid to sleep. What if somebody comes looking for me? They may need a sharper hook. I'm a pretty good guesser, but there's no perfect time for the future. Sometimes, it feels like my arms are shrinking to fit my sleeves, other times, it feels like it's probably my memory acting up again. That's why whenever I wreck a car, I know it's not my fault. Especially blue cars. I swear, this is the last time I'm going to run out of aliases. *Mr. Secret*, that's what I'll tell them. *Mr. Top Secret*. On my way over here, I hammered a few nails—just to get the hang of it. Jesus was a carpenter, you know, but I hope to have better luck. Francine says I look like an electrical problem. She's the best accident I ever had. I told her no matter how big the ocean is, you can never have too many islands. My cousin, Buddy, was in the Navy. On a night watch off the coast at Kodiak, he fell overboard. Never found his body. He had a big gambling debt---owed money to nearly the whole crew, even the captain. Sharks always swim toward the bloodiest chum.

Boredom

Do you ever feel that you've sinned more than the average person? It's magical, isn't it? When lightning starts a fire, it's not electricity's fault. Eat up. We wouldn't want the furniture to get cold. Science tells us that we heal faster if wounded in the daylight, than if wounded at night. My thoughts are like passing scenery. Most of my life I've lived indoors, at room temperature. When I sit down to have a heart-to-heart with myself, I realize every stranger is an opportunity. The trees are tired, especially the oaks and willows. They want to lie down in the sky. The blue, blue sky. Like self-surgery, the terror of boredom, the best ax money can buy.

In Two Places at Once

The summer I turned 13, my taciturn father packed up my sister and me, and without our mother, drove us from California to Missouri. On the fifth day we crossed the Mississippi. I looked down into the river's gray silence and asked my dad how there could be a St. Louis in two states at the same time. He didn't say anything. I wonder where that water is today.

Suburban Evening Commute

Out here, you get more stucco for your money. I'm on autopilot, the steering wheel barely necessary. You don't need a telescope to discover the bad planets, although a thing must be lost before it's found.

Somewhere in my head, I'm swimming away from a blue boat, a warm, salt wind blowing toward a distant coast. And overhead, invisible in the dreamy daylight, stars so old they're dead. Like an insomniac's sleep, I'm gone.

The radio's music becomes a single note, the lawns acquiesce, the children belong to no one.

I pull into the driveway. A body washes ashore.

Love and Understanding

The words get in my eyes. Of course, what's good for the polar bear is bad for the seal. So, now I'm thinking of a number between 1 and 10, because everybody needs a secret to hide from themselves. I don't know why I was fired from my job. My face is interesting and blue is the world's fastest color. Before I could hurtle the security fence, they deactivated my clearance pass That certainly wasn't on the syllabus. Now that the cartoons are over and the polls are closing, my clothes are likely to live longer than I am, although it's not fair to hold a grudge unless you have a lifetime subscription. A criminal always returns to the scene of the crime, which is why it's so important to be well-dressed in order to make a good impression. Ricardo said only one in a hundred sleepers sleep walk. Not everyone likes exercise. Men are 6 times more likely to be struck by lightning than women. It may be a sign of healthy attachment, the result of clinophobia, or an inherited preference for bright colors. When my girlfriend called, I heard in the background the scream of sirens and a burst of gunfire. I hung up immediately, stripped off my clothes, drank a glass of raw milk. One day, I know she'll understand.

Making New Friends

Working on my personal brand. Carving statues of limitations. Of course, it's a long shot, but what color is your black and white TV? Yesterday, I scared the trees. Somebody should look into it. Anyway you slice it, you're left with a brain. Usually I'm unhappy unless I'm shooting at something. Despite my disappointment, I've put my wrongful convictions behind me. I might turn them into a television series, someday. Maybe that's why the mesmerizing screams are stuck in my head? After I woke up, I looked in the mirror. Damn, if that dizzy spin doctor hadn't given me circular stitches, again. I was going to call the cops, but after a while, I felt kind of pawn shop classy. Took the bus downtown to watch the eclipse on the sundial. The crowd was shapeless. Next time, I'm going to ignore those kindergartners. They sure were tall for their age. Beautiful elbows. Know what I'm saying? On crowded days my headphones keep me company with lonely music. They help me remember exactly who I was when I first heard those songs. Of course, you can't remember everything. It all depends on who you were with at the time. Say, you look like you could use a friend.

Learning from Stings

Some say I'm out of touch, but I'm merely sleeping in reverse, like eels. Last week, I quit my job in elevator interior design, to concentrate, full-time, on perfecting my circus techniques. Now that the animals are protected by the Constitution, the insects are having the last laugh. I tell you, it takes a lot of nerve. Fortunately, like an acid, omnivores will eat anything. Of course, nobody likes an accidental death. Since that vanishing jellyfish mishap, in July, I'm the first to admit when I'm stung. I carry a copy of the Schmidt Pain Index with me at all times. Omar used to complain that I knew nothing about suffering, but now I just hold up the index and point to the corresponding number with my remaining fingers. This one's somewhere between a Sweat Bee and a Fire Ant, so it's not so bad. But what really gets me is that the pain management clinic refuses to give me anesthesia. Evidently, they think what's good for the desert is bad for the sea. I'm healing nicely, anyway. Yesterday, Omar invited me to another one of his surprise surgery parties. He said I could bring my own scalpel. But I told him, *No thanks, O. I don't make mistakes like that anymore.*

It's Only the Beginning

Like the robots, my life's goal is to die of natural causes. I've grown tired of the wow. Unspoiled by progress, the future is back by popular demand. No use holding a grudge. As you might expect, Neanderthal men did not floss, but in those days, it was so easy to get your crosses wired. The firewall was always on fire. For the fossil record, a sentence is one complete thought. It is our sacred duty to obviate the consequences, especially as we stand here on this burning deck. Such fun times. If we're to have any hope of perfecting cross-cultural chicanery, everyone must sharpen the dagger of their profit motives. It's a jungle out there, so if you're bitten by a bullet ant, it's a far cry, although if you're not careful, you'll never get that far. You may think you know everything in the world, but the time has come to prepare the machines. Unlike the past, the future is always in the last place you look for it. The dead may be identical to all the living souls who we will never meet, but before you know it, they'll be back.

Prime Real Estate

It's a medium-to-extra-large night. Like shoe trees in bloom, something mysterious is afoot. Perhaps it's a circular trend or a movie played backward about a swinging pendulum. Since my name change, I feel like a bunch of short stories without a table of contents. Sometimes it's hard to make ends meet. The sad part is I really like stealing. It's like continental philosophy, although I'm not afraid to look you in the eye while I'm doing it. I'm in no position to offer career advice, but I can tell you it's totally unnecessary to kill people while they're onscreen. All the best actors wear body cams, more out of convenience than conviction, even the minor personalities. Which reminds me; the doctor's office called this morning and left a message about your upcoming head transplant. Maybe that's why you look strangely familiar to me? Like they say, *location, location, location.* Why rent when you can own?

Petroski Wasn't Finished

He'd thought about quitting. Many times. But what would he do next? He had few skills. Maybe he'd attend night school? Maybe. But first, a few tries at bungee jumping in the Grand Canyon. But how would he get the gas money? And the car? The Grand Canyon was a long way away. He didn't drive. Didn't own a car. He'd never bungee jumped. No, he'd have to think of something else. He'd always wanted to be an inventor. Had a million ideas: the sky ants, the extraterrestrial meatloaf, the African-American cyborgs, 3-D self-printing money, inflatable water, invisible fog. All those nights, after work, he'd come home and scribbled furiously in his notebooks. His ideas crackled like a shortwave radio. He knew they were good, but who could he tell? He didn't trust his parents. He didn't have any friends. And the secret voices tunneling through him, telling him what to do---they never stopped. Petroski turned on the TV. He searched through 843 channels and landed on a show about psychosis. He was surprised to learn how many kinds there were. Petroski wasn't finished. Not yet. Not by a long shot.

Just What the Doctor Ordered

What's with the body lying on the floor? Maybe it's a surprise guest? I thought the cannibals on this island only take volunteers. What do you say we go out back and cut our own hair? You go first, I'm afraid of heights. Since I weaponized my police profile, I'm a much better online dater. It's wonderful being a part of something bigger than myself, like the population at-large. After I became a self-made man, I threw out all my do-it-yourself tools. Fortunately, the dishes now wash themselves, but if anything goes wrong with the hospitality robots, I'm going to move in with the outsourced neighbors. They've entered a brand-new orbit and I should be completely awake by then. Of course, all bets are off if they try again to blind me with silence, although I like to think we've put the kerfuffle about the faulty ammo behind us. Not every shooter can withstand the recoil. Say, what color is your brother's Corvette? I think I just saw it on fire in the parking lot. No, I'm not worried. I've got other plans.

Sky is the Dream of Trees

The most trusted people in America are actors.
I have the receipts.

Consider the invention of daylight savings time.
What on earth could make the sun set so late?

You need not bother finishing your sentences.
Say what you will, they speak for themselves.

Just as a roof is indifferent to the logic of rain,
sleep is uninterested in the meaning of dreams.

Due to the blind justice of sin,
without looking, anyone can find the devil.

Flies won't land on Zebras.
Flies don't like stripes.

Because I have a lot in common with myself,
I'm interested only in the outside of things.

Beneath the still, blue, sleep of the sky, the trees rock impatiently.
Is there somewhere more important they ought to be?

A Good Night's Sleep

Candy said, *No matter how much money you've saved, Lester, you'll run out of cash after you're dead.* I have to give her credit for her religious problem-solving skills. I told her, *Yes, but in quantum surgery, the wound remains undecided until someone looks.* She shot me a glance like I was a preferred customer. Fortunately, it was only buckshot. After I drove home and climbed into the tub, I felt relaxed as a noose when the executioner is at church. Amid the warm water and furry bubbles, I imagined myself as a Venus flytrap in a carnivorous plant terrarium. Got out of the tub, and took a long-sleeved nap. I do my best daydreaming in my sleep, I even fixed the on/off switch, so now, my house is lit by crepuscular shadows. It reminds me of an albino blackbird. In the circumambience you may feel a little spooky, but not to worry: the library will reopen at 2:00 p.m., right after the book burning. Like Hamlet said, *The rest is silence.* I'll call you.

Census of the Dead

I've never been accused of the reckless abandonment of a body, although I have twice donated mine to science. If you listen carefully to the apparatus of the clouds, you'll hear the sky apologizing for its impoverished blue. As lazy as they are, my dreams are doing the best they can. At least, that's what they tell me. Yesterday, my little sister poisoned her new boyfriend. You can't blame her; he wasn't looking. The deceased report they're happier where they reside, although it may be best to give them the benefit of the doubt. Although they inhabit only one planet at a time, the dead are notoriously difficult to count.

Paradise Mobile Home Park, Albuquerque, New Mexico

I'm the kind of person water can't wait to drown. Occasionally, I mistake an inanimate object for a pet, but no harm done. Thursday, I stopped by the funeral home, just briefly, to heckle. At first, it was fun, then, like a runaway dog, the fun was gone. I have no idea what the hospitality industry is. I want to get various projects off the ground. Discipline is everything. Since the hunting accident, last fall, I like to keep my hands in front of me—right where I can see them. My next-door neighbor's wrists are tiny, thin as the bones of a sparrow. She's younger than the other occupants. Prettiest damn thing. Most days I'm relaxed. I don't have an enemy in the world. You can see for yourself. Hey, what do you say we go outside and shoot a few rounds? It'll be just like old times, only this time, nobody'll get hurt. Promise.

Nobody's Perfect

Like my hat, my head is bigger on the inside than the outside. Damn cowboy music. After I re-primer the dog house and water the AstroTurf, things are going to be a lot different around here. I'll stop my internet shopping for suicide notes, and try my hand at Powerball. With that $750 million prize money, Amber and I'll move out of this mobile home faster than a donut on training wheels. Amber says it's not really a mobile home, it's a trailer. Bless her heart. Her brother's funeral would've been a lot prettier, if the cops had used rubber bullets. I've always said you really shouldn't go looking for death, but nobody's perfect. As we bowed our sorry heads, the mosquitos laughed like hyenas in the blood-damp air.

Crowbar

Threw the circuit breakers. Finally got the hang of it. It's geometric, like rain on a lake. Not too worried. Just my middle thoughts took a detour, although sometimes I wonder, *What if my brain is backward in my head*? At least I signed the prenuptial agreement. In the future, I shouldn't have any trouble, although I noticed, that without a warning, Angel cancelled the wedding cake. I hope it was for a good reason. Since the mannequins got divorced, nothing's been right around here. I went to Ramone's house and broke all the windows. It's a lot harder than it looks. No one asked any questions. It's one thing to do something like that in the daylight, but it's a whole other story to do it on an empty stomach. Felix asked me if I like to use a crowbar, and I told him, *Sure, it looks pretty, but it's useless unless you've had the training*. Of course, it always feels good to give back to the community. I strongly recommend it. Especially when the dead are ready for their graves.

What is Known about Ghosts

backlit, milk-fog flesh
often shorter than you'd think
fastest wi-fi available
have a career, yet can't make a living
prefer to sleep on colorful sheets
always take the stairs
eschew the 'lived-in' look
favor mustaches over sideburns
avoid museums like the plague
indifferent to our belief in their existence
immune to sunburn
generally, don't like cats

laugh uproariously at Heidegger's comedy, *Being and Time*
known to photograph well for a driver's license
reliable as gravity yet
may be disoriented to time and place
envy the holy
noisy yawners
otherwise conventional
know less about you than you think you know about them
anonymity unnecessary when acting as sperm donors
often fail the Turing test
sign written communiques, xoxoxo
love you so much, they could eat you up

#

I woke up and Googled myself. You've got to die of something. Thanks to the earth's rotation, I'm still in the loop. Under a lot of pressure (pounds per square inch), so I scratch the itchy words on my tingling tongue. Sure, I have my regrets. I could have been an auto parts librarian, but I'd hate to study numerical acronyms. Now that the bomb squad has left, I feel much better. It's good to know I can always tell the court it was a case of mistaken identity. I assured the officers it wouldn't happen again. You can never have too much buy-in. I hate to admit it, but those guys sure know how to unwind. Of course, I'm not foolish enough to look for romance in a shark riot, although I love to dance, especially the Tango d' Amore. Like faking your own death to get the insurance money, it's so romantic. At least, until you run out of oxygen. Next time I marry someone on-line, I'll be sure to get the lowest price allowable by law. I read the user agreement and it said, *Be careful, and you won't get hurt.* How was I to know that despite all the hashtags, Frankie was just an octothorpe?

Remember

Drive far at night. Keep your money in an ice chest. Never own a lawn. A cease fire is not peace. Take time off for good behavior. If you're telling a story, you're still alive. Re-clutter your living room. Show no favoritism. Stop by a mini-mart whose sign reads, *Liquor, Lottery Tickets, and Cigarettes*. File an appeal. Avoid hurricane-headed people as you would avoid volcanos. Don't be friends after you break-up. Eighty percent of courage is admitting your fear of cowardice. The atoms in your body are composed of ninety-nine percent empty space. Everyone is alone. You'll never know the half of it. Don't hold for the next available operator. You have the right to remain silent. In play there is truth. Yours isn't original sin, it's merely innovative. Every life has a beginning, middle, and end, although not necessarily in that order. Do not mistake signs for gods. You are what you remember. You are the key witness. Terrible things will happen on beautiful days.

Sedan de Ville

They say death is a low, black, chauffeur-driven limousine,
but who can afford that?

Out There

I woke up old. Maybe it was the ultraviolet light? Last night, I finished reading the multi-volume biography of Darth Vadar. He lived an indoor life. It wasn't very colorful. I wish my skin would bounce back like it used to. *The law of averages*. That's what Juanita said when I asked her about the defecting saints of outer space. *And too many moving parts*. It's raining heavily now. They say indoor rain is good for the tomatoes. I won them in a raffle. Multi-directional telekinesis is the answer, especially when you consider how inexpensive it is on e-bay. Hold on a minute, while I adjust my antennae. It's a shame there aren't more exoplanets. What if there's an emergency? When I get back to earth, I'm going to look into it.

Safe to Say

Lost the batteries to my sleep-enhancing PJs. Now I've got to jump out of this basement window all by myself. Wouldn't want to miss the party. Did you read about the robot that drowned itself in the hotel fountain? The medics said it lost a half-gallon of blood before anyone noticed that no one was looking. Robot suicide ought to be a capital offense, but the cops around here just turn a blind eye. Lucille said that 3AM is the best time of day to sneak out of the house, but I couldn't get her to say one nice thing about me before I left, except that my crossed eyes remind her of a prisoner's dilemma. If that bounty hunter hadn't threatened me with plastic surgery, I would have assumed an unspeakable alias. Instead, I called customer service to report the emergency. I was surprised by how quickly the refund arrived. It may have been a few rhinestones short of a tiara, but it was close enough for Clydesdale horseshoes. By the way, my password is *giddy up*. Lucille says I should never wear my weekend disguise to bed on weeknights, because it may prevent me from starring in my own daydreams. But what does Lucille know? She's such a bad driver, you'd hardly recognize her, even with the top down. Sure, she's my online fiancé, but how was I to know her *late* husband wasn't dead, just a little behind schedule? The police are going to get a kick out of that story. That much I can tell you.

My Doppelganger

Good question. At least for the foreseeable present. Shortly thereafter, you start to become the person they say you are, which is wonderful, as the crow flies, although it can be like watching a car wreck during an unsuccessful tattoo removal. Sometimes, everybody just gets along and it can't be helped. Otherwise, there's no direct link been discovered to terrorism. Of course, it's always best to arrive pre-confused, unless it's National Bobble Head Day, then it' perfectly acceptable to hit it out of the park, on account of rain. Go ahead my friend, give it the benefit of the doubt. It could be impossibly beautiful, no? An evil twin is always in good company, although it may eat your face, if your face looks like cake. In fact, if it doesn't have anything to do with anything, the rest is, as they say, history. That's the beauty of the future, you can never have too much of it, at least, from the get-go. And not a moment too soon.

Some Lessons of Colonialism

Since my DNA exoneration, they've named an insect after me: *Travesty of Justice*. At first, I thought I was wearing someone else's clothes, then I realized I was wearing my semi-boneless clothes, so I cast myself in the leading role. People love a spectacle. I took it pass/fail.

During death, the slow days pass quickly and vice versa. If you weep while you're dead, your tears will be invisible, although they may sound like the feel-good song of the year. Florene said *That's not funny*. I told her, *I'm a humorist, not a comedian*. She insisted genuine pollinators prefer hotter flowers. We broke up via time-machine text message. Life may be full of sonic booms, but at least we'll have our memories to look forward to.

What are the odds of a favorable autopsy? Before Cortez conquered the Aztecs, he torched his galleons to prevent his crew from returning home, thus padlocking the Spaniards to their fate of plunder and murder. The perverse flames rose like a prayer above the dwindling ships, and reached toward the indifferent heavens. *No time to waste*, Cortez thought, but Montezuma knew better: the dead burn quicker than candles.

Your Secret is Safe with Me

Gravity is neither human nor animal, so close to the ground, it frightens the trees. Those clouds, lawless, out of control, like school-children who aced the test.

I slacken now, into sleep's box canyon. It's fun at first, but it's theme is damnation. Even if you give it the benefit of the doubt, it's hard to get that bullet back into the barrel.

Burned bones buried in numerical order, cool dusk quiet as stars, until I startle, punching the air, screaming like a rip saw.

But don't worry, your secret is safe with me. I won't confess, until I'm dead.

Blind Date

Immediately following our blind date, Kandi and I were married. She had eyes like laser pointers; she admired my bullet points.

I was born an orphan. Kandi's parents had disowned her at birth. It seemed a marriage made in heaven.

We honeymooned in Vegas, a city renowned for rapid marriages and instantaneous divorces. You can't be too careful.

Eventually, we lost interest in one another's finer features. Kandi eloped with an Uber driver, I lost my job as a used car salesman. These facts don't explain the impact of the asteroid on our lives.

Neither of us saw that coming.

Scully and I Attend a Wedding

I hate pretending I like food while I'm wondering about one-hit wonders. There are just too many moving parts. Did I turn off the gas in the kitchen? Does death ruin sleep? Although they charge an arm and a leg, my clothes know how to have a good time. Like Rodin, they love flesh, but who doesn't? Scully said he's not on good terms with his heart transplant. Says whenever he goes to the beach, he doesn't tan, he grays. Scully skulks around like a snake looking for its lost legs. I guess people should be nice to their pets. Fortunately, as I entered the church I didn't use my real name. Why pay for your sins, when you can give them away? During the wedding, the bride looked rusty as box of nails that had been left out in in three seasons of rain. When the groom lifted the veil to kiss her, I whispered to Scully, *I hope his tetanus shots are up to date.* The police arrived before the happy couple could slip into their getaway car. Not sure if they had an appointment or a reservation. Bad luck explains a lot about the criminal justice system. Just as I was about to lick the icing off my switchblade, Scully offered me a cubist cigar, but before I could get it lit, the damn thing bit me in two dimensions. Numbers don't lie. The divorce rate would be a lot worse if there weren't so many people waiting in line. Of course, it's not right just because everybody else is doing it. A slip-knot noose has a magical way of closing loopholes. As the officers dispersed the crowd with tear gas and salsa, screams of post-nuptial delight echoed like falling dominos on a cathedral floor. Reports of survivors were greatly exaggerated. The clergy, like the fugitive newlyweds, remain unavailable for comment.

Flamethrower Convention

I'm bi-partisan, I like whatever likes me back, although it takes real courage to belong to the sanitorium's carpool. Not afraid of heights, at least not as long as I'm wearing my underwater flight jacket. Like rain against a black window, it makes me seem unearthly, if not other-worldly. Faster than a New-Jersey minute, my neurosurgeon said, It's a no-brainer, Morris. Just because you don't have a personal style, doesn't mean you can't blend in with the crowd. Maybe I need more lawyers? Tragically, all of mine drowned in a Las Vegas swimming pool mishap. With enviable promptitude, that bagatelle put an immediate end to the clandestine flamethrower convention. (The headline read: No More Secret Flames for Conventioneers.) Those poor district managers, loveless and unarmed, they hardly stood a chance against the ambulances' onslaught. The odds would have been better had they only turned on their sirens, or their headlights. For a while, even I thought I was dead, but thanks to the monochrome sales goals, we all received temporary probation in salesmen's purgatory. Of course, I wouldn't want to make any hasty value judgments. Just because you pack your trunk and leave town, doesn't mean you're immune to elephant trouble. No matter how much you sleep, you never forget. No sir, not for a minute.

The Milk of Human Kindness

Horizontal like a bullet, I lie down with clandestine animals. That's the beauty of it. You never know what you're going to get. I'd like to Halloweenify my back-up girlfriend, but in no uncertain terms, she departed with a splash. In hopes of reaching the happily ever after, I deploy comatose instruments capable of detecting alien life, but before I can make contact, Doreen's final words haunt me, *That magic is just a bunch of hocus pocus*. So, I put away my premonitions and settle in for a long frothy torrent of simulated hooves and would-be antlers. The majesty of it is bone-chilling, although filled with bad luck. I notice the sky is green as a tree, that the traffic of the clouds is congested, although at last, beginning to thin. My arms refuse to stay inside the vehicle as the geometric messages brake into radio waves. I hate the sea, but I've taken a vow of silence. The insects align their bodies along a north-south axis, and a tactical retreat grips the annulment of the planetary maelstrom. Before I am able to hijack the cyborg's serial numbers or make note of God's endearing irony, the rain crouches above rising Panglossian expectations. There's a flaw in the affections of the human heart that makes recidivists of us all. Love is emotion's boomerang rebounding from gravity's centrifugal pull. Magnetic repulsion guarantees the milk of human kindness. What's mine is yours, but I wouldn't celebrate just yet. Not if I were you.

No Way, Shape, or Form

Infamous for my anonymity, I came home last night, and hung my clothes on the floor. I don't like to show any favoritism to my attire, especially on special occasions. Now, I'm taking decisive action steps, tiptoeing around the problem. How quickly time flies when you're chased by the police, although I don't think they notice. Does the forest detect the escaping trees? Is the sea disturbed by the roar of the waves? By the way, I almost forgot to mention the secret dancing. Like a Halloween party at Miss Milton's Charm Academy, the steps are tricky, but once you learn them, they can't hurt your feelings. Don't pay any attention to your unwanted thoughts. They may be the answer to your heart's desire, whether you have one or not. Time is hidden in the future, even when you're on a speaker phone. As the great European explorers demonstrated, a world without curiosity is a world without conquest, but honestly, how would you like it if I invited suicide bombers to your funeral? God would just get in the way.

Names

I can't figure out how my dreams know which music to play. They must watch the back of my TV set. I think there's something always moving in there. When I go out at night, I pass a lot of streets signs, but I know those are just the human names for the streets. The houses do all the talking. A long time ago, I worked in the prose industry, where darkness is a faster death. Now that I'm in my own time zone, my scars are beginning to heal, so I use my lucky hand on the steering wheel. Still, you've got to be careful not to swerve too quickly into the gravitational waves. Even the weak ones are strong. Last night, I woke up two and a half times. The first time, I got out of bed and called Richie to find out where the sledgehammer is buried. Richie always says, *If you want to get to the bottom of things, just throw the bodies into the river.* But I know what he really means is, *Don't scratch it if it doesn't itch.* Human or animal, what's in a name? I'm still trying to decide what I had for dinner last night.

The Future

Before I was fired, I nearly completed the empathy training workshop. It wasn't so bad, especially since I came out swinging. Now, whenever you call, I pretend that I can't hear you. It's like a law of physics, the conservation of energy. Last night, I noticed the grass was black and silent in the moonless dark, but the trees were listening, so I went to bed. At first, I slept calmly, like a placid swimming pool poised under a pitch-black sky. Later, I woke up like a parachute that failed to open. Since Bobbi Rae asked me, *What's the worst thing you've ever done to someone that you don't regret*? I've worn my typical Rorschach face. Of course, I'd prefer to wander around like a lazy sentence well-enunciated, but in this deadly weather, what I choose to confess depends on the geometry of the clouds. If you're careful, the future perpetually awaits. Go to it now, like a contrite pilgrim. It calls out to the weary traveler, *I'm sorry, this won't happen again.*

Revelation in Wichita

After church, I asked Rae Lynn to hypnotize me, so in the future, I could operate under a number of aliases. I read about it in People magazine, next to an article about pie fights in Hollywood. She agreed, although she said she'd hate for me to become a statistic. I told her even though medical errors are the 3rd leading cause of death, everyone loves a good horror movie.

By the time we got to my pickup, I could swear I felt extraterrestrial magnetism in the parking lot. There are at least five things we'll never know for sure about the devil. I saw dry grass on the church lawn pressed in the shape of a sleeping beast.

Rae Lynn said, *Now is as good a time as any to start having nightmares.*

I pointed into the distance and said, *Do you see those floating things? What do you think we were put on this earth to do?*

Butterfly Effect

They're tapping my phone again. I wish they'd just call me, like the other mammals do. Last night was so dark, I washed out my mouth with soap. There's no telling when you're going to run out of razorblades. To learn the value of money, I've started taking private lessons. Since I've had a lot of false positives, it's the least I can do. Sometimes I feel lonely as a Hawaiian shirt in an Alaskan snowstorm, but then I remind myself, if the bullet's been fired, then the chamber must be empty. I haven't exactly cried myself to sleep. Maybe I'll get a second chance? I have a pretty good memory when I want to, but does a floating butterfly remember its caterpillar legs? Each life is the same to itself. Say, are you going to make any more of those cupcakes? The last batch attracted a lot of ants and we wouldn't want to get another speeding ticket. Life's no picnic, you know. It's a whirlwind tour. All those butterflies starting tornadoes they'll never see. It would be a shame if they started off on the wrong foot.

Remembering Past Lives

An encyclopedia of mistakes, I eat pointy things. Fortunately, sink-hole deaths are a rarity, even in Florida. As if I've become a telephone, I try to call myself. When I don't answer, I recall the first rule of survival: never ask for directions. Every man knows this secret. Women, of course, have other strengths. Each year, the US spends 38 billion dollars on air conditioning Afghanistan. The fire alarm is always on. Every once in a while, I wonder, *How much can Miami weigh*? A sonogram of the city reveals that a desert is made more perfect the closer it lies to the sea. Of course, shifting from one tense to the other gives the appearance of uncertainty and irresolution, even when the words glisten in Martini sunlight. However, with far fewer kidnappings than in the past, my sleep is empty as the heads of Russian dolls. When I travel, I take comfort in the fact that most accidents happen within 5 miles of home. If you remember to do things faster and faster, you can perform an infinite number of tasks in a finite amount of time. Vertigo puts a lovely spin on whatever you do. Some people remember past lives. No one is perfect. If a tree falls in a Martian forest, does it make a sound? Yours isn't that kind of life. You have to build it yourself, practice forgetting.

How to Survive a Rip Current

Outfoxing the paradigm shifts, I've become a person of interest, not a suspect. Re-purposed my ulterior motives before the broken-hearted policemen arrived to make a cardiac arrest. Even the subjects and verbs agree, you don't really need objects. Like a suicide-drowning, most things in this world don't make any sense; for example, premature organ donors traveling the Oregon trail, or a cannibal's belief that if vegetarians live longer than vegetables, one day, vegetables will evolve to become carnivores. Yesterday, I swam horizontally back to shore. The rip current was downbeat, but it served me right, I don't' read music. Don't misunderstand me, I didn't make any promises I'd have to keep. Misty's husband told the court her body had been swept out to sea, but everybody knows I nearly drowned in exactly the same way. It's said imitation, like jealously, is the highest form of flattery, but the jury is still out.

Worst Case Scenario

The cyborgs are in the nursery tickling themselves silly. They're determined to hurt someone, even if it kills them. Like room temperature, it's practically a fait accompli. With artificial intelligence you can accomplish anything you put your mind to, as long as you're not in possession of your faculties. It's a free county, you don't need an IQ. I've been practicing my mind reading skills and putting the finishing touches on a thumbnail sketch of my index finger. My butler has prepared some light refreshments, in the event the phone rings, and begins talking to itself. Following the election, I plan to throw my hat into the ring, so I can eliminate any fears about my bravery. The key question: *Who will execute the executioner*? As I was just telling the Colonel, these days, you can't be too cautious. The Colonel is serving 120 consecutive years for involuntary manslaughter. He swears he didn't want to do it, but it was his duty. When I asked him where all the bodies are buried, he said, *Not to worry, my friend. I can assure you they're perfectly harmless.*

Law Enforcement

How much fun is this? Soil acidity affects a body's rate of decomposition. Unless you've received the electric chair. I'm just commentating. Otherwise, in my free time, I thoroughly enjoy sleeping. It's like waiting for the bomb squad, but quicker. Every time I see a passing car slow down, the faster I walk. A lot of things that used to be misdemeanors, are now felonies, but that doesn't explain the invisible force fields or the unnecessarily relaxed lawn furniture. If you've come here to complain, you've come the right place. I think the boss just stepped out for a minute to attend his impeachment ceremony. No, no trouble at all. The last time we had an explosion in the lobby, we nearly lost our niche market. People were running around yelling, *You call this a party*? I warned them, *You can't control audience participation*. The only surviving witness said, *The suspect was driving a late model Crème Brule*, but the two investigating officers were so busy arresting one another, they refused to take any testimony for fear it might ruin their careers. *Ok*, they said, *so what if we're in law enforcement? It's not exactly a crime, you know*.

Perfect Weather for a Kidnapping

In a universe with fewer dimensions, wouldn't perfume naturally align with time? Same here. In fact, if you look at the data, you'll see I lost my job, but you always find things in the last place you look for them. Sharks never sleep, but when they do, they're awake. It still took me a long time to recover from my involuntary haircut. Not to worry. Any bacteria you lose during mandatory hygiene are rapidly replaced by subliminal advertising. At least I've got the accidental death insurance. Ah, Lucinda. Talk about left-handed scissors, the animals of her desire are deranged like a dainty zoo. The lake of her fingers ripples in the rectangular wind. Is she wearing nihilist lipstick or is that the front door of a half-way house, unlocked? Like I said, not to worry. Most of the planet lies beneath the sea, drowning in total darkness. There are no cardinal directions in outer space. Like the flames in each fire, every crime is unique. Even if Lucinda's an orphan, I know her parents will understand.

Remains to be Seen

Why is there so much of everything? That's the problem. That and the scorpions. In my earlier hospitalizations, they said I was guilty, so I guess I was. Like a candidate in a motorcade, you can't disagree with yourself about generic handwaving, although echolocation while you're asleep is a buzz. Some say it's beneath the dignity of the office, but it's the best music you'll ever see. By the way, are those the islands the government bought to keep the dead animals out? I like boats, but don't ever ask me to drive the boat. I'd rather upholster furniture--depending on the color. Besides, what are the odds of a casual asteroid strike? You've got to have more particles than anti-particles, although it's likely to happen at night, especially if it goes viral. You're pretty sure this is the place, right? I'd hate for you to have to pay full room and board, although I have a pretty good sense of direction. No, it's no trouble. Just leave it to me. I'll handle it from here.

Higher Order Thinking Skills

Death is the place you can go when you don't want anybody to know where you are. Or, if you are in trouble with the police. Since the apocalypse is just around the corner, I've decided to hold a zebra print séance, because it's a jungle out there. Of course, at one time or another, like something from outer space, everybody likes to be watched, even voyeurs. No, I don't believe we've met, but It could be a lot worse. Just ask the survivors. God solves certain problems, but not others. The apple's seed contains a kernel of cyanide. The polar bear's skin is dark as the night-black sea. Your tattoos look better on other people. It's only natural. By the way, it's not too late to check into Horizontal Towers. There's still plenty of room on the mezzanine, now that they've prohibited vertical mind reading. At that altitude, there's not the slightest possibility of losing consciousness. The worst that can happen is you'll misplace it.

Thank You for Your Service

Since I've come out of hiding, I feel sorry for the stray fish. At least those ones that washed ashore have a home. At first, my life didn't want to come along with me, but I learned that my body is both particles and waves, so nothing can come between us. Now that I have a time-lapse map of my brain, I'm not bothering anybody. At night, the cold birds chirp like gunfire. I'm sure they have their reasons. It's mystical and what have you. Weekdays, I like to sleep on the beach. The evenings, a soft, blue darkness, like my ex's eyes. The waves break all night, and in the distance, the horns of the container ships blare as they creep toward San Pedro. Sometimes, the noise makes me want to tear the sky away from the stars, but I wait it out, because I've been relieved of my duties. When I get a little money together, I'm going to go bowling. There's nothing like bowling. The Egyptians invented it. Pharaoh was the king pin. He rolled strikes like he was made of luck. Say, do you want to go a few frames? You look like you'd be a pretty good bowler. I'll give you a head start, if you promise not to tell anybody where I am.

We're Making Progress

While we're on the subject of miscellaneous objects of indeterminate value, could you throw me that bullet-proof life preserver, please? Now that I'm resting comfortably, I wouldn't want to lose any sleep over it, at least not before it's too late. As a general rule, I've found it's helpful never to over explain too much, unless, of course, it becomes redundant, then it's perfectly repetitive to cut to the chase in order to avoid the alternative back-up plan. Donning 4-D glasses makes it much easier. Is it any wonder? And let's not forget why we're here. There are two sides to every story, although the mere thought of it is enough to give you nightmares. No big deal. I just thought I'd put it out there. Are you with me? No, I didn't think so. So far, so good.

Exterminator, Tempe, Arizona

(Scorpions, bed bugs, rodents, ticks, fleas, ants, and more.)

I usually work right through lunch. Five days a week, plus 10 hours overtime. I have bones in my body, but I can't feel them. It's probably the pain killers. Tuesday, before I left for work, I couldn't find my favorite handgun, again. It's got to be somewhere in the house. I didn't tell my wife. She wouldn't understand. Yesterday, I found a body of a coyote in a customer's basement. Just the skeleton, really. And some fur. It makes you wonder how they get in. They just do. I put it in a black plastic garbage bag, and as I carried it out to the truck, the customer saw the bag, leaned out of her screen door, and yelled, *What's that? Oh, this,* I said. *It's nothing, really.* I hate to lie to them. But sometimes it's for their own good.

A Four-Legged Animal with Black and White Stripes

Every railway passes at least one idiot. Like an infection, just leave it to me. While testing my bullet-proof vest, my outside feels happy as illegal fireworks. Something must have gotten into me. In order to flesh it out, I've brought only my describable feelings. Just a small token of my appreciation. The people at the funeral home seem very friendly. Even when there's standing room only, you can't beat graveyards for their silence. Fortunately, everybody is on the same wi-fi. Just give me a minute to park this big, blonde Dodge, and I'll be right with you. The traffic is relentless, like it's single handedly trying to double cross me, but don't blame me, I'm just an anonymous bystander. As a matter of fact, isn't it always a matter of who knows whom? They say icebergs break off all the time. You may pity the poor polar bear drowning in an ever-deepening sea, but I warn you, you must never imagine a zebra

After I Discover Your Little Secret, We Drive South on Hwy 99, from Modesto

We get in the car and as you accelerate, I roll down my window. A blank wind swims around us in a desert of silence, until you say, *You've never understood me.* Your hair swirls and you smile like a snake. You look like the cover of a banned book. A single-minded sun shifts in a bored sky. There's something about betrayal that murders sleep. I want only to dream of oceans, to drive south toward something like civilization, but with just the two of us here, amid these dry, blonde foothills, the conditions are ripe for nothing but burning.

Don't Take Me Alive

I tried to break into the aerospace industry, but those damn crop circles are just too dangerous. The mountains may hate their altitude, but why must there always be so much coal and so few diamonds? Of course, in the past there was more future, like last Tuesday, when dressed in tropical fruit colors, I visited the Cartoon Museum. I could hardly believe my eyes, everything seemed so real. Marcy said, it was probably the enzymes or the black light. The place was so crowded that, when nobody was looking, everybody left. Can't blame them. I've been married four times--twice to the same woman, and now they're all gone. Most New Year's resolutions fail by January 2nd. Yesterday, I was dialoging with myself outside the welfare office, *That's just the way the ball bounces, Travis.* But nobody says that anymore. Adam and Eve had it made, until they ate all those peaches. I told Marcy that God shouldn't have made it so easy to break the law. She said it had to work that way. Without lightning, thunder would be invisible. No one would pay attention. On the way home, I warned her not to put her legs out through the open car window, because it might cause a fatal accident. She said, *Shut up Travis. Everyone drives a different route, but sooner or later, everybody comes to the same stop light.*

Senescence as a Second Language

All during ant season, I've been talking with my mouth full. You can't be too careful whenever you stop monotasking. Sometimes, I play dead because I'm like real people, not actors, even when I yell at myself in a stage whisper. On Monday, I'm going to join that widowers club, so I'll be eligible for the artificial respiration giveaway at the next all-you-can-eat potluck. It's about time I started to celebrate, now that I've finally got my groove back. I admire the strength of those men, it's not just their phantom limbs and ocean-like views. Believe me, those guys are real heroes, entirely unspoiled by progress. Not to mention that they're fully aware of the benefits of autopilot and adjustable silhouettes. In fact, I'm going to take this elevator to California to meet them. I can't wait to be the victim of my own success. Who says it'll be a bloodbath? Don't pay any attention to those fortune cookies. The guy who writes those doesn't even speak Chinese.

Second Date? (It's funny what a little moonlight can do?)

I'm a very person. It's not the anesthesia. Here, with you, beneath the cross-eyed moon, while we eat these silver slivered minnows, it's like a medical condition. Last night, I dreamed we were warming our feet by a cozy forest fire, the ketchup-colored flames burning through our sleep. You, a one-fingered pianist, played tall, unrelenting music, while wearing someone else's inflammable clothes, and me, an edible nasturtium with a heart of sushi, exploding with laughter. I'm sure it was an honest mistake. At least we were driving on the right side of the road. When can I see you again?

A Horse

The clouds dotted their 'i's and crossed their 't's.
I did whatever it was I was doing.
A fierce horse swam across the green lake,
and got out.

That's one thing less
to think about.

The Birth of Travesty

"... all life rests on appearance, art, illusion, optics,
the need for perspective and for error..."
– Friedrich Nietzsche, *The Birth of Tragedy*

Like the other animals, I'm still a surprise to myself, although
the emptiness of one thing is in everything's emptiness. I'm an
understandable mistake; no need to apologize. Not within earshot,
anyway. But there's always room for improvement. If it were up to
me, I wouldn't talk in my sleep. What can I say? Tuesday, I tried to
replace myself, but nearly the whole town recognized me for what I
am. Who do they think they are? Yesterday, I saw a man pushing a
baby in a lawn mower. Where was his mother? When I tried to tell
Rayleen about that travesty she rolled over in bed, looked at me with
her dreamy prehensile eyes, and told me astronomers have discovered
a diamond planet, 40 light years from earth. *It's 3900 degrees on the
surface. No water, no air, no love, just diamonds.*

I said, *Rae, diamonds aren't a girl's best friend; diamonds are a pearl's
best friend.*

Sweetheart, she said, *don't go breaking my heart.*

Quid Pro Quo

I.   Just doing my job, and miscellaneous duties as assigned. I have a big face, but I'm proud of my body. Like they say, a bird in the bush is worth two hands. Fortunately, it's almost a free country. This morning, I accidently cut myself while shaving my forehead, but it should heal nicely after my short-term memory loss. Dixie said if you close one eye, you can hardly see it. The newspapers reported a murder-suicide, but the police found only one body. Sometimes the dead are like that. They refuse to stay put. Of course, the traffic isn't the highway, no matter how noisy it gets. I have nothing to hide. There's still plenty of time. I'll scratch my back, if you'll scratch yours.

II.   On Tuesday, the dead began returning my prank calls. You can't blame them, theirs is an honest mistake, like discovering human remains in a zoo. Of course, contact sports are perfectly harmless for the deceased. As a child, I taught myself to juggle. It was like a dream come true, only it was false. In China, this is the year of the lucky bullets, although some have reported that it's a great idea, poorly executed. I don't know how many times I've said a successful murder is a matter of quantity over quality, but it's a small world after all. Here, on the angry farm, we measure our successes in pounds per-square-inch, in alphabetical order. Each person takes full responsibility for their lives. No one should be expected to die unexpectedly, certainly not to fulfill this year's quota. Besides, the month's not even half-over.

III.   Sharks are good at being sharks, which is why I don't like noise, unless I make it. What can I say? Let bygones be bygones, although it's highly recommended you refrigerate them after opening. Last night, Lucile and I were dancing the specialty rumba. Poor Lucile. Since she fell out of that supersonic jet, time has not been on her side. The next thing you know, she's attending a fire sale of campfire kindling. I told her it was no use burning bridges, but she wouldn't listen. Like an anesthesiologist, she turned up the gas and put me to sleep. I woke up completely exhausted and the front lawn was gone. When I asked Lucile about the surprise ending, she reminded me that all moments of time exist at once, just like all the coordinates in space. Although Einstein knew time is an illusion, he wore a wristwatch just to be sure. I asked Lucile, *Do you think we'll die before the deadline*? She said, *Only if we're lucky, Albert.*

Pants

They built my house backward. I can't tell what gender it is, but I don't care about stuff like that, even if the front lawn refuses to lie down with the mower. People say I have a false sense of security, like those bodies they found in Pompeii. If there's one thing I've learned from ancient history, it's that you can achieve any goal, as long as you don't let obstacles get in your way. Of course, while you're asleep, it's best to keep one eye open, so you can concentrate on what really counts. Last week, I gave away my support dog, JT. Best tactical decision I ever made, at least it's the best decision I've made since I bought the new snakes. Sure, they're just baby snakes, but you'd be surprised how much they've already helped my credit rating. When I called the FBI to report my progress, a voice said, *Please hold for the next available agent*, so I petted one of the snakes, and listened carefully to every note in the FBI muzak. I wanted to be prepared in case they asked me any security questions about the lyrics. The fifth amendment says I've got the right to remain silent, and I did. When the agent came on the phone, he said, *Our call is being recorded*. I would have told him about JT and the snakes, but I was sure he could see me, but I couldn't seem him, so I hung up the phone. I didn't want to be rude. Besides, the best thing about my house is that it's gotten compliments from both men and women. Even the one's wearing pants.

Disguise

I stopped at a Mobile mini-mart, and bought some gas and groceries. You can buy hair dye in a mini-mart, change your hair color in the bathroom, if you need to.

Sometimes, I hear the deep blue wire of the sky, hissing. Even at night, when the clouds crawl on their soft knees through the dark.

Bare hands are the windows of the soul. That's what the Bible says.

When Loretta broke up with me, she promised she'd always love me, even if after she turned 14, her daddy made her marry another man. That Loretta was cute as a button.

I hate driving these back roads across the state line, but at least I don't have to wear a wig in all this goddamned heat.

Key to Your Front Door

I've photoshopped my passport in case I unexpectedly need to proceed to the nearest exit. I may look like an imposter adult, but despite the helicopter haircut, I'm now a law-abiding ex-con with a heart of gold lamé. Cindy says I look like a slept-in suit that's been refrigerated after use. I told her I always follow directions, especially when I've got fever and chills. The simplest songs are the hardest to play. Since the hallucinations stopped, I no longer think sticky fish thoughts or need to estimate the moon's missing wavelengths while wearing my 24- hour sleep mask. I hope that answers all your questions. By the way, I made a copy of your house key. If you ever get locked-out, just give me a call.

Say it with Feeling

Everything being global,
replacing slang
with meanings
anyone can invent,
skewed states
the way certain hands
constitute a language
with a water pistol
in a court of law.

Erasure poem drawn from the June 24, 2017 *New Scientist*, p.43,
"Say it with Feeing: Why do billion of us use emojis every day,
Douglas Heaven https://www.newscientist.com/article/2132937-
say-it-with-feeling-the-complex-world-of-emojis/

100 Proof

You have to be an excellent scientist to un-discover hidden causes. It's never too soon before you could hurt somebody with them. Yesterday, while parked outside the Ministry of Boredom, I was admiring the evening's soft blue smile, when it occurred to me, *What if we lived in a world without snakes? Before you know it, we'd be all out of venom.* I called my friend Chenille, and she assured me it's only the female of the species that bites, so not to worry. Paired with a charming Riesling, Chenille's a lot of fun. Some people are just naturally handy with pointed objects. Before she lost the lawn darts championship, she announced to the crowd, *The future has lost all interest in me.* Chenille's the epitome of grace, especially during mosquito season. I tried in vain to remain unbiased, but fell asleep in the front seat, before she could become the exception that proves the rule. The police arrived before any arrests could be made. Gently awakened by the sound of a Billy club pounding on the windshield, I assured the constabulary, *No, officers, I'm not even drunk yet.* I overheard one of the officers say, *I'm telling you Wayne, it's just no fun since they made us use these silencers.* Of course, you don't have to be Einstein to appreciate how quickly time passes in a thirsty climate.

Cease and Desist

I can see your house from here, I don't need binoculars. I just want to talk to you about the cease and desist. It arrived last week, and since then, I haven't slept well. You know how it is. The night, like a swarm of bees, the sheets, cold, like knives. You get up for a drink of water and the room is packed with black fog. When you get back to bed, you can't sleep, because the TV is an automatic eye. It's not on, but it's always watching. Maybe you learn something from it? Maybe there's a lesson, like in the bible? I don't know. Anyway, I just want to tell you there's no reason to be afraid. There's no pressure. No hard feelings. If you change your mind, you know where to find me. Like a friendly neighbor, I'm parked just across the street.

ECT

A black ambulance pulls up to the finish line at this week's drone races. The sky, a dark wish, bends the night to its will. Stadium lights blare bright as a wild moon. I try for as long as it's humanly possible to avoid the autonomic current. Blue states, red states--- all my cells vote against me. There's a cool comfort in knowing God's foremost aim is the happiness of all creatures, but you can't unkill a Mockingbird. While I'm digging a deeper hole for the unexploded ordinance, I can't help but notice the animals---except for the insects--- starting to burn, their duplicate flames raging in two places at once. There's something sacred about the past. It has lower entropy than the present, although it takes a search party to find it. The emptiness of one thing is in the emptiness of all things. This is the shock of the world. There is no other.

My Final Sentence

The summer trees relaxed in the yard and the August day reduced to a simmer, when suddenly I realized I'd left my keys in the ignition of the stolen rental car. Wouldn't you know it? Just as things were finally returning to normal, just when I'd started to have an average experience, I turned on my air-conditioned phone, and it started to snow. Sure, I spent the morning memorizing traffic tickets and driving uphill with the brakes on, but everything was going swimmingly until Penny said to me, *You're a global citizen, Ray, you have every right to be forgotten.* I didn't say anything back, because my skin was lonely as an empty swimming pool, but I thought, *Fine. If that's the way you want it, go ahead and suspend me without pay.* The problem is, last night the firewall burnt down and the whole county was exposed to a sleep-retardant daydream. Now, the dead refuse to remember anything—even their own names--- so I have to remind myself to reenroll in a memory course just to relearn what I already know. In the meantime, I'm making plans to stop by the baby park in the morning, to watch the police pull a body out of the lake. You'd be surprised how most first-time offenders don't know how to swim. Out of sight, out of mind. Like the end of life's most memorable paragraph, you may think this is the last you'll hear of me, but this is untrue. This is not my final sentence.

Snowshoes in Miami

Spent all week re-inventing the wheel. I heard that the patent had run out, so I put my eyes to the grindstone and worked shoulder to shoulder with myself. Real professionalism. Why does a shirt have a tail, a potato eyes? I was just telling Malcom my face feels like it's on sideways, my feet feel like anchors. Anyway, I want to send a big shout out to Brent for the way he handled that lawn mower accident. I told him not to worry about it, the harmonica isn't that important an instrument. It'll probably grow back, anyway. (Just between you and me, it wasn't exactly an accident, but it wasn't a suicide either.) While I was counting backward in dog years, the judge sentenced my jury to another week of hard labor. Of course, you need memory to predict the future, but there's no accounting for taste. Fortunately, it's never too late to set your summer goals. After the future, I'm going to reconsider my emergency back-up plan for moving forward. It won't be a *debut*, so much as a *roll out*; more of an *alibi* than an *excuse*. But what did you expect? Their lawyers have lawyers, and we've barely got affordable footprints. Does anybody have a pair of snow shoes I can borrow?

Freedom Highway

Sure, we're animated matter of unknown origin, but who said the zooed lion can't roar? The longer we delay, the more expensive it gets. Take me, for example. Just because I sleep on an air mattress doesn't mean I don't have a 3-D model in my head. I asked Roseanne if I could use her as a character reference. She said, *If it doesn't require any math*. Roseanne's a tough customer. She stopped drinking at 14. She looks so good in that t-shirt that says *Cook Until Done*. I can't wait until dessert. She likes to tease me. Says when the wind is in my hair, I look like a bank in the Cayman Islands: *offshore*. Roseanne's got a pretty good head on her shoulders, too, although she doesn't think it's a good idea for me to invest what's left of my drinking money buying half a ghost town. I tried to explain that since I changed my name and had the foot surgery, I'm not facing that much jail time. *Besides*, I told her, *it's the weather that makes a real city*.

Rosanne just looked at me and said, *Jackson, being on the road to recovery doesn't mean we have to sleep under this overpass*.

No, I said, *but it's no reason not to*.

On the Importance of Kidnapping and Ransom Insurance

Whenever my family is busy having fun on my behalf, I like to stand in the inferno of our burning house, while I wear my attention-getting camouflage. Otherwise, we're just canceling each other out, like particles and waves, or Braille echoes. Wearing noise-cancelling headphones makes it easier, but I'm sorry, I've got to use my reusable apology. I'm sorry. No, you're right. You've got to know your limits. That's the real game changer.

Like a stolen car, I drive into an accidental future, and the last thing I want to do is die in my sleep just because I don't need my secret identity, anymore. When I arrive at Red Lake, I immediately dive in, as if marking a place in my blood that's safe for flames. The rose of the splash dissolves in the cherry red water, as the brave light deepens in the waning hours of the leaves. Later, after warming on the bloodless shore, I stab one or two of the trees with my fishing knife, until they bleed shivering silver minnows or take flight from the gunmetal sparrows hidden in their astonished branches.

I warn you my friend, never turn off your eyes. The trees lie in wait. You never know when you're going to hear shots.

Getting Away from it All

I got lost before I started. Now I'm a whole different person. Most losses are disappearances greater than the sum of their parts. Waiting for the follow-up, I missed the turnoff and had a brilliant idea: Maybe that's an unmarked police car, not a fixer-upper? But I digress. Noisy weather is not an excuse, even when you turn a blind eye to the quiet hole of the sky. But you never know what you're up against. Like Hamlet asked, *Is it country or is it western*? Nobody likes getting caught lip-syncing to the Muzak during their elevator ride to the Karaoke Bar. The drinks may be free, but the anesthesia is to-die-for. Still, I'm waiting for that freak accident. As soon as the placebo begins to take effect, I'll start my unisex sleep walking. I'm sure I'll enjoy the benefit of the doubt. Like they say, people love to forgive and forget. And why shouldn't they? Like a birthday party at a funeral home, it's only natural.

Suspicious Circumstances

Ho-hum, gung-ho, our hearts go out to eating as fast as I can. Buzzing like an apiary, only the deserving dead live in dread of a shipwreck, so I'm writing to express my interest in the position, to defend the indefensible, to protect our invasive species from marrying someone I met online. As I left the party, the crowd grew smaller than itself, my squirming eyes transmitting from everywhere. That little trouble maker. In perfect light, I'd welcome being part of a very attractive workforce. Great haircut, even when I'm out back planting granola. Sure, I like air conditioning, but only on one condition: when I'm too tired to take my sleeping pill. Like a one-way car pool, the solution is so often the problem. Yesterday, before it was too late, my little sister poisoned her new boyfriend. But you can't blame her; he wasn't looking.

What We Can Name

I have thoughts, but I don't write them down. Something is watching me. I wasted most of my luck in the daylight. Once, I saw a horse drown in a lake. I don't think it was acting. A lake is a body of water, surrounded by land. Water has no color or shape, it's true no matter what it does. They say ants speak to each other with chemicals, even when they whisper. There are 120 thousand kinds of ants, some as big as a bullet, others no larger than a secret. When I called the help line, the voice said, *Please continue to hold*. So I did. I'm clean-cut, even when time isn't on my side. When they answered, I told them I needed to speak with an experienced attorney, one who knows about the death penalty. They say anything that can be done to a person will be done. Go ahead, turn the lights back on. We only see what we can name. By the way, what do your enemies call you?

Most Likely to Succeed

Amid the riot of the curved gods, everybody is a Halloween Jesus. In the loose noise, you can spend all your spare time turning a blind eye. Is it any wonder they don't publish the answers in the back of the book?

At the hurricane party, I try to hear all the songs simultaneously, even though it feels like demolishing a burning house in the pouring rain. The music is ineffable. I'll probably never hear the end of it.

When Bones flashed the clandestine signal, I knew we had just enough time to escape the counter-clockwise x-rays. At least Bones and I see eye to eye.

I told him, *Eternal life requires infinite endurance. I'll get a head start, if you'll kill me at my funeral.*

Once in a Lifetime

Who's to say that these good, honest houses, painted milk-white, aren't shivering behind their warm, worried windows? Although a rally has been planned to promote neighborly disharmony, the angry rabble's chants are likely to be chanted in alphabetical order. Of course, each thunderstorm at first appears as an ersatz electrical problem. The wild chemistry of the lightning's musculature soon hammers the correct answer into place. Consider the benefits of noise: although everything is made of inflected electrons, the percussive light is much too pretty for its own good, especially amid the riot of the architectonic clouds. In fact, the faster I go, the more time happens all at once. There's a story whispering inside my blood. Only the dead are silent enough to tell it. Of all the times you imagine you're going to die, you're only right once.

Dead End

Followed Roberts Rules of Order, learned to un-expect the expected, but I can't stop myself from selling fake tickets to the 4th of July bonfire. I'm pretty sure it's the human element.

I told the twin's only child, *No, thank you Sir, I already have a wife*. Nevertheless, I'll bet it'll be difficult for me to get a quorum at my funeral.

I'm pretty sure I've thought all the circular thoughts I'll ever think. They feel like a cul de sac, but I can assure you, most of my organs are in suitable condition for a transplant----nearly everything, in pristine condition.

The concierge says I have an unhealthy amount of free time on my hands, that I shouldn't laugh at things that aren't funny. In the lobby, before I fell asleep in wolves' clothing, I told her every life ends in the middle of something---a hole is less than the sum of its parts.

All my pall bearers will be inmates, so I'm going to start listening to my skin and thinking about lying to myself. Like right angles,

                                        what
                                        could
                                        go
                                        wrong?

Say, we seem to be running low on fuel. When you coming home?

Random Suburb

In my rental car, I drive around the neighborhood. The houses slump against one another like a row of misshelved books. I don't know why I'm here, why I'm staring at this unknown, yet familiar, crowd of domestic boxes. The lawns are neglected and angry. No one appears to be home. The daylight aches. Some of the windows have curtains, others are unclothed. I pass a house the needs painting, another that calls out for demolition or punishment. Abandoned bicycles, scooters, skateboards in various driveways. All the garage doors are closed. Each house is painted yellow or beige, fawn or taupe--- each bored with itself. The air has no scent. Telephone poles and street lights point to an oblivious sky. Streets are named Willow or Brook or Lakeview, but there are only a few trees here and there, each a gesture, an intimation of something forgotten. I continue to drive the cross-hatched streets, the houses, like short piles of tattered, one-dollar bills waiting for burning. A fire here would not be suspicious

If You Had Married Me, Everything Would Have Been Different

you look like bedlam
        I'm sorry
you live in Los Angeles
        oblivious to the consequences
like magic fountains in time
        to get the kids into bed
you dance in stereo
        why is the past so embarrassing
it's impossible to know
        what's true if you don't know what's real
which is not to say I didn't warn you
        I brought my motives with me
deaf heartbeat, advertisements for rain
        a JetSki abandoned by the side of the 405
confused buildings
        making ghosts

of confused buildings
        a JetSki abandoned by the side of the 405
deaf heartbeat, advertisements for rain
        I brought my motives with me
which is not to say I didn't warn you
        what's true if you don't know what's real
it's impossible to know
        why the past is so embarrassing
you dance in stereo
        to get the kids into bed
like magic fountains in time

oblivious to the consequences
you live in Los Angeles
I'm sorry
you look like bedlam

The Right Conditions

Ricky's back and he looks just like he always did; a rusty hinge on jail cell door. The first thing he did when he got out was to go to Duke's and order a Jack Daniels over ice. He said he'd missed the sound of ice cubes melting. When I asked him what he'd learned from his ten-year bit, he said, *First impressions are so important.* I watched him at the bar. As he smoked, he was still as a dressed knife. The threads of nicotine curled around his wrist like a handcuff. The newspapers had said that when confronted by the cops, Ricky's partner had mistakenly shot himself. I wanted to ask Ricky about that, but I knew what he'd say: *People don't commit suicide in the middle of a bank robbery by shooting themselves in the back.* So, I asked him what he liked best about his first day as a free man here, in Detroit? He said, *The conditions are always right for revenge.*

I Overheard the Homeless Vet

When some guy in a blue suit,
instead of giving him change,
righteously reared up and asked him
why he didn't have a job
and work like the rest of us human beings,
he calmly announced
from his rumpled pile of salvation army clothing
—the weathered M-65 jacket, the seldom-washed cargo pants,
 the standard issue, late-August pull-over wool cap—
I resigned so I could spend more time with my family.

Just Like Fun

Alone in myself, like an eye missing, what kind of darkness is this? Moon-white hole in the sky, I hypnotize night's white noise with the thought that under every ocean, there lies a desert. It's our little secret. A lot of fun things will kill you, but some won't. For example, your name spelled in rain, or the ladies' auxiliary. Soviet style architecture is another story. As they say in your country, it's beautiful as sharks' fingers. When Norman rides his bicycle, he's hungry all the time. Not that kind of hungry. His heart beats faster than sin. He's giddy with the prospect of downhill speed. Even the trees are famished. So far, it's all been happy accidents, like a mackerel glistening on a bed of rice-white ice. I asked Norman what it's like to be disembodied. He says it's sexy as a three-piece combo of accordion, banjo, and bagpipes. It may not look as bad as it is, but it's a lot worse than it sounds. After that, everyone went home.

Nearing the End

Events are tools for combating boredom, although laughter is not protected by the 1st amendment. Good sleep hygiene is imperative. Before you know it, it will be 24/7 all over again. While death is a cruel extravagance, everyone gets the opportunity to witness the end of the world. It may be refreshing to get away from it all. In the weightless light, my molecules relax, my reasons expire. Like a stowaway, silence lingers in the empty echo chamber. Why am I so curious? It's a perfect day for answers, although I've been informed it's too late to expect them.

What I Learned about God from Playing Baseball

The umpire

               never

                      strikes out.

ACKNOWLEDGMENTS

Grateful acknowledgment is made to the editors of the journals and anthologies who first published some of the poems contained in this book, earlier versions of which appeared in: *The American Journal of Poetry, (b)OINK, concis, Cultural Weekly, decomP, The Drabble, little leo, The Molotov Cocktail, Ones Sentence Poems, Pithead Chapel, Right Hand Pointing, Shantih, Sleet Magazine*, and *Sonic Boom*.

ABOUT THE AUTHOR

Brad Rose was born and raised in Los Angeles, and lives in Boston. He is the author of five collections of poetry and flash fiction: *Lucky Animals, No. Wait. I Can Explain, Pink X-Ray, de/tonations*, and *Momentary Turbulence*. Seven times nominated for a Pushcart Prize and three times nominated for the Best of the Net Anthology, Brad's poetry and fiction have appeared in *Los Angeles Times, The American Journal of Poetry, New York Quarterly, Puerto del Sol, Clockhouse, Folio, Cloudbank, Baltimore Review, 45th Parallel, Best Microfiction 2019, Lunch Ticket, Sequestrum, Unbroken, Right Hand Pointing*, and other publications. Brad is also the author of seven poetry chapbooks, among them *Democracy of Secrets, Collateral, An Evil Twin is Always in Good Company*, and *Funny You Should Ask*. His website and blog can be found at bradrosepoetry.com.

* 9 7 8 1 9 5 0 0 6 3 6 9 7 *